Grandma's Silent Auction
January

Michael James

Copyright © 2020 by MICHAEL JAMES

All rights reserved.

No part of this book may be reproduced in any form or by any electronic or mechanical means, including information storage and retrieval systems, without written permission from the author, except for the use of brief quotations in a book review.

CHAPTER ONE
CIARA

I have my very own clothing boutique outside of the city. I design most of the clothing myself. I grew up around the clothing industry. The famously known MV clothing brand was started by my grandma, Milli Verbank. She made a name for herself and I have the same ambition as her. I started studying fashion at a very young age. I became obsessed once my grandma dragged me along to a fashion show. I was probably five or six at the time. After that is when I started spending my weekends drawing designs, messing with fabrics and draping materials over a mannequin instead of playing with dolls. If I had a girlfriend over for a sleepover, I always dressed her up for a fashion show.

Looking back at it today, my sketchbook holds many horrible drawings. Half of them I have no idea what they were supposed to be. I remember my grandma always telling me they were wonderful designs. I hold onto those drawings for the simple fact that my grandma stood behind me. She never once discouraged me and that is a blessing in itself. She built my confidence over the years without her noticing. She doesn't take any credit for leading me into the fashion world, but she should.

Although my grandma and I share a love for designing, making, and selling our line of clothing, we don't share the same opinions in much else. For example; she thinks I should have my boutique inside the city. I don't like the city. She believes I should vote, but I don't really understand politics so why bother. She thinks I should separate myself from my old friends because they aren't rich. Her belief is that rich people are the ones who buy designer clothes, not the poor. If the poor do it's because it was a gift or found at a second-hand shop. *'The rich are the ones who advertise your brand,'* she always says. I, on the other hand, think anyone who wears my clothing is advertising the MV brand. Since she has stepped away and is enjoying retirement, she doesn't realize that I don't just cater to the rich anymore. I have a line that I call the more "affordable rack". It's not made any cheaper, I just cut the price willingly. I am barely making any money off it, but five dollars is a profit in my eyes.

I am minding my own business, hanging the new shipment on the rack when Porter gets my attention. *"Psst,"* I look up and he's by the front window. *"The eagle has landed."* I giggle. *"Oh, boy, there is not one, but two limousines."*

"She's just here to pick up the dress, so don't stress."

The door chimes as her bodyguard opened the front door. My grandma has money and she likes to flaunt it. She wears a black hat with white fur around the edge. It matches perfectly with her white fur coat. Her sunglasses are dark and too big for her face. I giggle to myself when she whips them off her face.

"Darling, why are you doing the racks while he watches out the window? You do too much on your own."

"I'm fine, Grandma."

She glances around my boutique as she takes off her leather gloves. She snaps her fingers at Porter, wanting him to take her coat. He hurried over to be her servant. I go to her to give her a hug.

"I am so very excited for this evening. Hurry up, Ciara, and show me this dress for the silent action."

"It's in the back, I'll go and get it."

"You are not just going to bring it out on a hanger, are you? You must model it for me."

"Why? It's not like I'm wearing it."

"Do you need help getting into it?" I shake my head no. *"Scoot, we don't have all day."*

I shook my head no for saying I don't want to put it on! However since I have not seen it on a human body, it might be best to try it on. I take the dress out of the protective plastic bag. Damn, I did a hell of a job on this gown. It took me two months to get it the way I envisioned. I love it. The dark red is eye-catching. The front is very revealing, at both top and bottom while the back adds to its total beauty. The fabric is soft and elegant. The price tag would scream MV if it were going on the sale's floor.

I slip into the dress and go out to the showroom. My grandma claps her hands in excitement. *"You, my sweet girl are going to be the talk of the party. Every girl there is going to wish she were you. Every man is going to be wishing he was the one to kiss you when the clock strikes midnight."*

"Grams, I am not wearing this dress to the New Year's Eve party. It's for the silent action."

"You, my dear are wearing it." She opens her purse and hands me an envelope. *"This is your itinerary for the rest of the day. I'll see you later at the*

party." She snaps her fingers at Porter again. He gets her coat and holds it open. *"Don't disappoint me, Ciara."* I frown. I don't want to wear this dress.

The second my grandma goes out of the front entrance and the door is shut, Porter is ripping the envelope out of my hands. He reads it out loud. *"Spa, lucky girl. Nails, hair, makeup, blah blah! Oh dear, you are not going to like the next one."*

"What is it?"

"Waxing the works! Ouch for you."

"What else?"

"Take Porter with you!" I roll my eyes. *"Just kidding."*

"No, you're not. You know damn well I'm not going alone. Put the closed sign in the window while I get changed."

When I arrive at grandma's mansion, the driver helps me out of the car. Porter is a smart ass and holds out his arm for me to take. We reach the door and the butler lets us in without question. We don't need to check-in as he knows who I am. I stop anyway. I need to know if Hunter has shown up yet.

"Samual, has Hunter Bloom arrived yet?"

"No, Ma'am he hasn't. I don't see him on the guest list."

"Well, put him on it. He's my boyfriend."

"Yes, Ma'am."

Porter and I check out the silent auction before entering the backyard where my grandma had outdone herself on setting up the party tent. Even though it's the last day of December, it's warm inside. I give my coat to the attendant before going in further.

"Money can get you anything. You'd never know this was a tent. Look at that stage! The dance floor is probably better than the floors in my apartment. A live band! If I forget to mention it later, this is the best New Year's Eve party I've ever attended."

"You think that's impressive, wait until the fireworks go off at midnight."

Porter sticks to my side all evening, thank God. I haven't seen Hunter at all. I've called and texted him and he hasn't responded back. I have no idea why he hasn't shown up yet. He knew this night was important to me with my dress being in the auction. My grandma does this party every year, but I never wanted to do the auction before. It hurts he has stood me up and is ignoring me. We've been together a year, you'd think he'd have respect for my feelings and tell me he didn't want to come. I would have understood since he doesn't like Grams and she really doesn't like him.

Porter and I have eaten a lot of finger foods, consumed our share of alcoholic beverages and cut up the dance floor for the past few hours. It's almost midnight. My grandma's bodyguard comes to me and drags me away. All he said was it's time for the auction.

I stand beside the stage as Grams walks out to the microphone. *"Ladies and gentlemen, thank you all for coming tonight and for the generosity with your donations. Let's get right to it!"*

She waits for the applause from the crowd to calm down. I stand here with knots in my stomach. I have to parade myself out there in this dress in front of hundreds of people. I hope it raised enough money for the knots to go away.

Grandma announced all the winners. I wasn't paying much attention until Porter taps my shoulder. I go out on stage when she calls my name. Don't trip, Ciara goes through my mind until I'm standing right next to her.

"As some of you know we held an auction for my granddaughter, Ciara's designer evening gown." She

stops talking again for applause. *"With the bid of three-thousand and four-hundred dollars, William Stone is the winner of this lovely dress. It's one of a kind."* She laughs. *"I sure hope it's for that beautiful wife of yours!"* Wow, my dress made the most money. That's exciting. I am about to walk off the stage when my Grams grabs my hand. *"Now for the results of the other silent auction."* My head snaps when I quickly look at Grams. What is she talking about? *"There are ten lucky men who get to date my granddaughter, Ciara."* Huh? What the fuck is she talking about?

I free my hand from hers and run off stage. How could she do this to me? She knows I am with Hunter. Porter calls out my name, but I keep walking away as fast as I can with these damn heels. I get to the exit and Grams bodyguard stops me. I try to push past him but he isn't letting me go.

"I have instructions to take you into the house. Millie will be right in."

I stop fighting him. *"Good because she's about to get a piece of my mind."* I look at Porter. *"You are coming with me. I may need backup."*

"Why would your grandmother do this to you?"

"I have no idea. It's probably because she hates Hunter."

*"Did you hear those names she dropped? Some of

these guys are very well-known. They are rich, and high profile men, Ciara."

"Exactly why I don't want to date them. Does Grams really think I'm dating ten different men? That is what she meant, right?"

"Yes, darling that is what I meant. Porter, if you'll excuse us, I need time with Ciara alone." I frown when he leaves. He's supposed to be my backup. "Let's have a seat."

"What the hell were you thinking when you went behind my back to play cupid? I have a boyfriend, Grams."

"I'm thinking about your future, Ciara. That boy you are dating is not Verbank material. It's time you find a man suitable to be your husband. I am not getting any younger and I need to know who will take care of you after I'm gone."

"I think I have plenty of time before you die. I think I'm capable of finding my own husband. How do you know if I want to marry Hunter or not? You have never asked."

"Do you want to marry that boy?"

"Yes, I do, someday."

"If you marry that boy, I will strip you of the MV branding and all the money that goes with it. I will not allow my beautiful, smart granddaughter to marry *a gold digger. He wants you for the wrong reasons and not for the right reason."*

"What do you consider the right reason? Power, money or a known name?"

"Love, Ciara. Hunter doesn't love you."

"How do you know? You don't even talk to him!"

"And where is he tonight?"

I lie. *"He got held up at work."*

"Is that what he told you?" She goes over to her desk. She gets her tablet. I want to run and cry when I see the screen. *"Work, huh? It looks more like a college party to me."*

I finally sit down before I fall down. No wonder he didn't show. Happy goddamn new year to me. These weren't the fireworks I was talking about with Porter.

"You are taking the next twelve months off from work. You will date each man for one month. You will only communicate with the man you are dating in that month. When November hits, you will pick who you want to marry and have a December wedding."

"And if I don't?"

"Your inheritance will go to charity. I'm sorry, Ciara, but I have no choice. I need to know you will be taken care of when I leave this world. These men are good men. I did background checks on them all. I

spoke with their ex-girlfriends to know they treat women well. I'll give you until seven in the morning for your decision."

She leaves and I burst into tears. How can she do this to me? I cannot believe this is the grandma who raised me. I don't care about money. I can make my own. My dress tonight proved that. My sales for the last ten years are evidence enough. I can stand on my own two feet. I don't know what to do. My Grams means the world to me.

CHAPTER TWO
CIARA

I ran from my Grandma's mansion as fast as I could last night. How could she do this to me? Putting me in her silent auction like I'm a cow ready for slaughter. I am flabbergasted she'd do this to me. I truly don't understand the meaning behind it. Yeah, I get she doesn't like Hunter, but that isn't a reason to put my heart in her game. You are not supposed to play games with people's hearts, let alone their lives. It's just wrong.

I've always held my grandmother high on a pedestal. She demanded respect and I gave it to her freely. After all, she earned it over all the years of being my family, my friend, and my mentor. She took me under her wing and kept me safe when my mother's wings were broken. I am so hurt that Grams would do this. My heart truly hurts. It's not about the

MV branding, the money, and all the materialistic shit! It's about respect and my freedom to love who I want. She doesn't have to like, talk or associate herself in any way with Hunter. She just needs to let me be with who I want.

Porter chased after me and hopped into the limousine with me last night. I wanted to be alone. He wasn't having it. He sat next to me rubbing my back while I cried into his lap. He didn't try to talk me into going along with Grams scheming ways. He was just there for moral support by sitting next to me, letting me deal with things my way. When I got the bright idea to find Hunter and confront him, Porter didn't try and talk me out of it, even though I could tell he thought it was a bad idea. When Hunter was nowhere to be found, we went back to my apartment above my boutique. I cried some more. Hell, I cried until the sun came up. It wasn't until it was close to the time I had to meet with Grams that he asked his first question. *"What are you going to do?"* I told him the only answer I knew. *"I don't know."*

Here it is seven in the morning and I'm arriving at Grams. I still don't know what I'm going to do. The car pulls up in front of her mansion. The driver she sent for me puts the car in park, then comes to let me out. I walk up to her front steps with puffy, blurry eyes. The butler is there ready to greet me as always. He tells me where I should go to meet Grams. I want to scream. I get halfway to the kitchen and I want to turn around and run. Somehow my feet keep moving in the direction of the kitchen, though.

I enter the kitchen and Grams is at the breakfast table having her tea and whole wheat toast. It's always the same breakfast for her. When she hears my footsteps on her marbled flooring she looks at me. I think my appearance shocks her. I don't really care if she doesn't like my messy bun, puffy eyes and cheap, fuzzy pajamas. Let's not forget about my slippers that desperately need to be replaced.

"Come, sit and have some tea."

I plop down in the empty seat across from her. I put my elbow on the table and lean my chin on my hand.

"What flavor tea are you having, Ms. Verbank?"

"I won't be having tea. How about a whiskey on the rocks!"

Grams isn't happy with me. Good because I'm not happy with her, either. *"She'll have Chamomile."*

Just because I feel rebellious I say, *"I'll have Saffron, thanks."*

"I take it you did not sleep last night!"

"No, Grams, I did not. It was quite difficult after being auctioned off at the beef cattle farm."

"Oh, stop it, Ciara, you act like this is a horrible thing. Have you once stopped and thought about the adventure and the possibility of finding the love of your life?"

"No, because I already have a boyfriend whom I love."

"You mean the thirty-five year old at a college party last night, that one?"

"If you are talking about Hunter, then yes, that one!"

The servant puts my tea on the table. *"Would you like a muffin? They were baked this morning for you."*

"No, thank you."

"Box them up for her please, Kate."

"Will do, Ma'am."

"Ciara, you know I've always given you the freedom to be who you want. I have never overstepped, even when I didn't always agree with your choices. You work long crazy hours. I get that because you learned it from me. Now that retirement has set in, I realized how much fun I missed out on. You are young and vibrant, still. It's time you let loose *and see everything that is out there. Honestly, there's a world full of stuff to do besides fashion."*

"You didn't need to sell my soul for me to do other things."

"Sweetheart, the adventures are more fun when you do them with someone you love."

"Grams, I don't love these men. I don't even know who the fuck they are."

"You watch your mouth in my home!"

"I am dying to know something. How much was the price tag to date me for a month?"

"That doesn't matter. It went to charity."

"Were all ten men the highest bidders?"

"Yes, but they also are the ones I had at the top of my list."

"How many, Grams, how many wanted to buy me?"

"Fifty-five." I cover my face with my hands. *"You're a hot item to sell. I had to put a limit on how many. I do wish to see you marry this decade."*

"Do you hear yourself? You are proud of how many men wanted to purchase me as if my earrings are a price tag dangling from my ear. You are losing your goddamn mind."

"I am proud that decent men want you. You are a remarkable young lady that deserves the best. These

men are the best. I didn't just pick any guy off the tree, I made sure not to touch the rotten apples, so to speak."

"Oh my God, Grandma."

"I've wanted the best for you since the moment you were born. Just because you are an adult doesn't mean that stops. I have never steered you wrong before and I'm not starting now. Just trust me, and have some fun. Take each adventure as it comes. If you find love along the way, who cares how you were led there."

"By adventures do you mean fuck each guy?" Take that, Grams!

"Ciara Mae Verbank, you are not too old to get that mouth of yours washed out with soap." She wiggles in her seat like she's Blanche from the Golden Girls. Her voice changes as well. "What you do in bed and with whom is nobody's damn business."

"So, I have your blessing to have sex with all ten? Duly noted, Grams. So, when do the adventures begin? I'm sexually deprived."

She rolls her eyes. "Your plane leaves at noon."

I jump up from the table. "What?"

"Sweetheart, sit down. Life is short and there's a world out there ready for you to explore. I wrote down *everything you need to know."* She gets up and gets a plastic three-ring binder from the counter. She opens it, puts on her reading glasses, and starts reading. *"You are flying off to California where you will meet, Denise Gibavic at the airport. She is Malcolm Miller's assistant. She will be taking you to his home."*

"Who is Malcolm Miller?"

"Your boyfriend for a month."

"What does he do and why did you pick him?"

"He's a white hat hacker. He's super intelligent."

"A geeky nerd, thanks, Grams!"

"But wait until you see him. Meow!"

"Sounds like you should adventure with him while I run my store."

"Nonsense. He wouldn't know what to do with this cougar." Grams laughs and I can't help but laugh too. *"We best get you cleaned up. You have a plane to catch."*

"I have packing to do."

"No, you don't. Isn't this great, Malcolm is taking you shopping. In fact, they all are. You are luggage free for the next ten months!"

I cover my face with my hands again. My fingers part and I peek at my Grandma through them. She is sitting across from me with a giant smile on her face.

I can't believe I'm doing this. I must be as crazy as she is. Grams best hope is that this nerdy dude is worth my time. The beginning could be the end of Grandma's game if I absolutely hate it more than I already do.

CHAPTER THREE
MALCOLM

I spend most of my days and nights working. If I'm not working, I'm probably just enjoying a night out with some friends. I tend to lay low. I'm not a person who likes the club scene anymore. I did when I was younger, but not so much now. One day I told myself it was time to buckle down and grow up. I did that by working hard. I made a name for myself and became one of the best damn white hat hackers there is. The problem with working long hours and being as dedicated as I am, it doesn't leave much room for dating. I do want to have someone to come home to after a long day of work. I want those kids that jump up and down because daddy came home. I keep telling myself to relax a little and find that one special girl. I made myself a lot of money. I don't need to pull the long hours that I do. Yet, I haven't slowed down at all.

I was working a fourteen hour day when my mother came to see me. She wasn't too thrilled with me because I missed the dinner she had planned the weekend before. My work interfered with her dinner. She put a gift box on my desk and slid it closer to me. It wasn't Christmas yet nor was it my birthday. She told me to open it with much excitement in her voice. I opened the box and took out a portfolio. That's when I saw Ciara Verbank for the first time. My mother explained to me that Ciara's grandmother is doing a silent auction. At first I couldn't believe what I was hearing. That's ludacris, who would do that? I told my mother there was no way I was partaking in such a thing. What person in their right mind would bid on a woman just to spend a month with her. I wasn't that hard up for dates. I slid the portfolio back across my desk.

"Malcolm, you need to start thinking about finding a wife. All you do is work."

"I'm not going to find a wife by dating her for a month. And why is it only a month, anyway?"

"Because you won't be the only one bidding on her. Millie is taking ten men's bids."

"Wait a minute, let me get this clear. If I win, I get her for a month then she goes off to be with someone else?"

"Yeah, I guess."

"What's wrong with the girl?"

"Nothing, Malcolm! Millie just wants her to find love. She's like you all work and no play."

"I'm sorry, Mom, but I won't be doing this."

"Why not? What do you have to lose?"

"Have you thought about if I end up liking the girl? Where does that leave my feelings when she leaves to go off and date some other dude? I sure as hell don't want to sit here and lick my wounds because she left."

"But you'll never know if she's the one if you don't try. She could pick you in the end."

"Mom, if I'm the first guy, there are nine more men behind me ready to dazzle her. Nine months with other men."

"If it's true love, sweetie, nine whatever's won't matter. She'll come back if the love is real. What if she falls in love with you and you don't love her back. It's a risk for everyone involved, including her."

"Sorry, I'm not doing this."

My mother didn't stick around much longer after that. She left disappointed that I wouldn't bid on some girl. She left the portfolio on my desk. I picked it up and put it in a drawer. It wasn't until three days later that I took it back out and started reading everything inside. I couldn't deny that she's a gorgeous woman. She's independently wealthy and a workaholic like myself. I wondered why she agreed to date ten men. Why not less or make it a full twelve. That's when I found the reason. Ciara has one month to choose which man she wants to be with and then have a December wedding. That's the moment I started thinking about the possibility of love and marriage. My mom was right, it could be me. I question myself if this would work. At the end of the day, I couldn't do it. I put that gift my mother gave back in the drawer. I left work and went home. I couldn't sleep that night. I couldn't put my finger on what was nagging at me. The next day. I went to my office at five in the morning. I took one last look at everything inside the portfolio. There it was in the middle, the charity. The charity is something close to my heart. I didn't hesitate, I picked up the phone and dialed the number. I listened to the directions and gave my reply. I didn't know if I bid high enough, at that second it didn't much matter. I gave my donation. I hung up the phone, thinking about what I did. Pleased with myself that I gave to charity and actually excited that I might get to know Ciara.

That was three weeks ago. Today is the day that Ciara arrives. I am the first guy. I didn't want to be the first. If I like Ciara, I'm going to need to leave a lasting impression on her. Nine months is a long time to forget all about me. It's a long time for me to sit and wait to see if she wants to be with me as well. I was hoping to be somewhere in the middle. It is what it is. I have to make the best of it.

I woke up this morning and got dressed as normal. When I was done getting dressed, I looked at myself in the mirror. Maybe jeans and a t-shirt isn't what I should wear. I'm going for that lasting impression after all. I get a sweater from my closet and put that on instead. There, that's better. I trade out my converse for combat boots. I'm not sure what look I'm going for. Fashion isn't my thing. Ciara might have a field day with my wardrobe. If I don't get the girl, at least I might get some style.

Before I leave for work I check the guest bedroom one last time. I'm not really sure why. I had my cleaner make up the room yesterday. There's new bedding on that bed because I have never had it set up before. No one's ever used the room before. The room had furniture in it since I moved in, but that's as far as I ever got with it.

I leave the door open on my way out. I grab my laptop bag off the kitchen island and head out. I would have loved to greet Ciara myself, but I have work that I must attend to. I had it scheduled before I bought a girlfriend for a month.

CHAPTER FOUR
CIARA

For the life of me I can't figure out why I am on this plane ready to go meet some guy who bought me for a month. Grams made sure I was on this plane to California. I am sure I could have outrun her once we got to the airport, but I didn't even try. What does that say about me? Am I that lonely? Do I not love Hunter as I thought or is it payback for him ghosting me? I haven't figured out why I'm doing this. Maybe I am bored with my life. I work long hours. When Hunter and I are together it's basically Netflix movies and a pizza. We have sex occasionally and then he goes home. He rarely ever spends the entire night with me.

My flight is only a few hours long. I have my earbuds in because I am not getting stuck in a conversation with the person next to me. I make sure my seatbelt is tight. I am not a big fan of flying. I'm good once I'm in the air, but the take off always spikes my anxiety. I should have bought a book in the bookstore. At least that would have kept my mind a little busy for takeoff.

"I just love flying!" The woman next to me says.

I have two options here, one I could ignore her because clearly she doesn't see my earbuds or two, answer her. That could lead to a full-blown conversation that I don't want to have. I don't like being a bitch to people, but i'm not really in the mood for chit chatting.

I move the cord to my earbuds, hoping she's paying attention. Ugh, goddamn it.

"I don't care for it."

"Oh, are you nervous?"

"A little bit." I giggle. I have this habit of giggling when I'm pissed off, being sarcastic or feeling I'm being verbally attacked.

"You should put some music on, put your head back, close your eyes, and picture being somewhere you've always wanted to go."

I giggle again. *"You are totally right."* I show her my earbuds and put them in.

She taps me on the arm. *"You need to put your phone in airplane mode."*

"I did, this isn't hooked to my phone." Gosh, I'm not an idiot. I just don't like flying.

"Okay, I just wanted to make sure."

I give her a thumbs up. This flight can't end quickly enough. Sadly, we haven't even left land.

Now that I'm back on the ground, I wish I were back in the air. I have to walk through the terminal and find a lady holding a sign with my name on it. I follow the rest of the people and start looking for where I have to go. I have never done this on my own before. I have always traveled with my Grandma or Porter. I just tagged along with them. Now I wish I had paid more attention.

I see people up ahead meeting their loved one, friends or whatever they are. I start looking for the lady. When I don't see her, I follow the signs for the information desk. I don't have to bother with getting my luggage as I don't have any.

I spot the lady. She sees me and smiles. *"Ciara Verbank?"*

"Hello, Denise Gibavic, right?"

"Yes! How was the flight?"

"It was alright."

"Good to hear. Are you ready to get out of here?"

"I am."

"Great, our car is waiting."

I walk beside her and watch her out of the corner of my eye. I don't want her to know I have no idea what the hell I'm doing. We get outside, and sure enough, the car is waiting. We get into a town car and Denise offers me a drink. I could use one to settle my nerves, but I decline. She then tells me Mr. Miller is at the office and we'll be going there first.

"How far away is that?"

"Half an hour if traffic doesn't slow us down."

A million little questions start entering my mind. Who is Malcolm? What is wrong with him that he pays for a month long girlfriend? Is he leaving the office when we get there? Do I call him Malcolm or Mr. Miller?

"You know what? I changed my mind, I'll have a drink after all."

"Nerves setting in?"

"Oh, no they set in a while ago, they are just intensified now."

She laughs. *"Mr. Miller is a cool guy. He's very laid back. I'm sure you two will get along just fine. Just don't let his intelligence intimidate you."*

"I know nothing about him besides his name and occupation."

"Oh! I guess you are going into this as a blind date." She giggles.

That's it? I was fishing for info here. Isn't there like some girl code here? C'mon, Denise, give me the goods! Tell me all about my blind date.

She gets on her phone. I can't help but wonder if it's about me. She is reporting back to her boss? Is she telling him I am not worth the money he spent on me? Good god, maybe she's telling him I'm not his cup of tea. I hate this. I hate that I have to do this all over again in a month. I'm going to have a nervous breakdown by the time I'm done with this bullshit Grams is putting me through.

"I let Mr. Miller know we will be there shortly. He's looking forward to meeting you."

"Why did he do this?"

"That my dear is a question you will have to ask him."

I turn my head and watch out the window. I hold this drink in my hand that I haven't touched. I don't think my nerves could handle anything in my stomach right now. I would be embarrassed if I had to run to the restroom and vomit. That would not make for a very good first impression. I briefly look at Denise.

She sits quietly next to me, doing something on her phone again. It's the first time I really have taken in her appearance. She wears jean capri pants, a white blouse with white tennis shoes. Her outfit is surprising for being an assistant. I would have thought she'd be a little more dressed up. This tells me, maybe Malcolm is cool as she said he is.

It gets dark in the car. I take a gander at where we are. Denise touches my hand that is squeezing the seat. *"Relax. Malcolm isn't going to bite."* She laughs. *"For now at least."* She smiles. Yes, I caught what that comment was intended to say. I just smile back.

We enter the building and a woman at the first desk says hello to Denise. Meanwhile, her eyeballs are ogling me. I take it everyone must know I am with Malcolm. We take an elevator up one level.

"Mr. Miller prefers taking the stairs. He put in the elevator just for me because I have a bad knee."

"That was considerate."

"See, he's a nice guy. He won't bite."

She knocks on his door before entering. *"Mr. Miller, how are you today?"*

"I'm good, Denise."

I get a good look at Mr. Miller and all I can think, what the hell was Grams thinking! This guy is old enough to be my father. I'm dating a q-tip for a month! This is not happening.

"*Hello,*" he says to me.

My mouth is suddenly dry. I clear my throat. "*Hello.*"

"*This is Ciara Verbank. We are stopping in to see Malcolm.*" My head snaps. What? This isn't Malcolm? Who is this?

"*Malcolm went down the hall, something about the printer.*"

I let out a breath of air. Gee, give me a heart attack. Grams was just about to get one hell of an earful. "*Hello, Ciara, it's a pleasure to finally meet you.*"

Grams was right, meow! Hello, Mr. Miller. Shit I meant to say that out loud. "*Hello, Mr. Miller.*"

"*Call me Malcolm, please.*" I smile. "*I just need about five minutes with my father, then we can sit and talk. If that's alright with you.*"

"*That's fine. We have a full month to talk, right?*" That was a very dumb thing to say. Get a grip Ciara!

Malcolm winks at me! Damn, was that panty melting. I would fan myself if Denise wasn't staring at me. "*Why don't you come have a seat? Would you like a drink of water, tea, or coffee while you wait?*"

"*Got anything stronger?*"

"Mr. Miller might have a bottle of wine around here somewhere."

"Water is fine."

She leaves me alone in Malcolm's office. Is it bad that my curiosity is going rampant and I want to look through his stuff? I better sit down on the love seat before my hands start being nosy. Has it been five minutes yet? I spot a door and I wonder if it's a restroom. I haven't had a chance to freshen up yet. I walk softly across the floor as if I'm a kid that doesn't want to be yelled at for snooping. I get my hand on the knob, ready to open it.

"Are you looking for an escape already?"

Shit! *"No,"* I shake my head. *"I figured this might be a restroom."*

"Well, you guessed right." He smiles and winks at me again. This might be a very long month. I don't date men as good-looking as he is. *"Did you need to use it or just checking the place out?"*

"Oh, I... definitely need to use it."

He snickers and I quickly get the door open and lock myself inside, putting my back to the door. Get a grip, Ciara. You are making yourself look like a fool. I rush over to the sink. I turn the water on, ready to cool myself off. I stop. I don't have any makeup with me if I smudge what I do have on. I turn the water off.

I catch a glimpse of myself in the mirror. Good god, my clothes are wrinkled from the flight. There's nothing I can do about it without having luggage. I tell myself, *"put your big girl pants on and go talk to the man waiting for you. Stop trying to find reasons to stall."* I unlock the door and exit the bathroom.

Malcolm is leaning on his desk with a tablet in his hands. I walk toward him. When he notices me, he places it on his desk. He stands and reaches out a hand. *"Hi, I'm Malcolm Miller."*

"Hi, I'm Ciara Verbank."

"Let's have a seat." We sit on the love seat. *"How was your flight?"*

"It was okay."

"I have an unexpected meeting in an hour. I asked Denise to take you shopping, if you aren't too tired."

"I do need clothes unless I want to sleep in my birthday suit." Please tell me I didn't say that out loud!

"I prefer to sleep that way, but if you feel the need for sleepwear I guess shopping it is." My expression must say it all. He laughs. *"I do own some. I suppose I'll have to wear them when we have breakfast."*

I swallow. *"How long is your meeting?"*

"A couple of hours I'm afraid. We'll meet up at my home later."

"Okay."

Malcolm gets up, goes to his desk and gets his wallet from one of the drawers. He comes back to where I am and hands me his black credit card. *"Buy whatever you need. Tomorrow we will be attending a formal dinner. A cocktail dress will be needed."*

"I have my own money."

"That's not part of the rules."

"What do you mean? I'm not allowed to use my own money?"

"No, you're not."

"Why?"

"Because I can take care of all your needs and so can the others. Your grandmother wants to show you we are willing to give you everything your heart desires."

"I can do that for myself."

"I'm sure you can. It's not about that. It's about showing you security. Financially being stable is just one thing we can all offer you."

"So you know the rest of the guys?"

"Some."

"Why did you do this?"

"It's a great charity."

"Oh!"

He laughs. *"Because I think you are beautiful and*

I couldn't help but wanting to know you." His phone rings. *"Excuse me."*

I keep my eyes on him going to his desk. By that I mean on his ass. I watch him talk to whoever is on the other line. I am surprised by the way he is dressed. He wears black jeans and a gray polo style sweater with a little zipper at the collar. He has on combat boots that are loosely tied. I would have thought a business man as he is would be in a suit and tie.

Malcolm announces he has to get to his meeting. He holds out a hand for me to take as I get to my feet. He leans in and kisses my cheek. *"I'll see you at home."*

That sounded weird to hear a man say. *"See you in awhile. Are we staying in or dining out?"*

"Denise made us reservations at Twelve Al' Dente."

"Italian?"

"It's the best place to eat near my home. I have to go." I nod my head.

I wait for Denise to come back. That didn't go too bad, right? He seems like a guy I could get along with.

CHAPTER FIVE
CIARA

Denise has brought me to the mall. Since she couldn't find anything stronger than coffee at the office we had a drink in the car. I think I like this car with a mini bar in it. I gotta tell ya after meeting Malcolm, I really needed a drink to calm my nerves. He seems like a laid-back, cool guy so it's not that, that had me sweating bullets. It's his hot factor that has me flustered. I felt like a complete idiot in front of him. Another thing that has rattled my cage is taking his credit card. I am not a needy person. I am an independent woman who doesn't need him to take care of me. And that goes for the other nine guys. I felt cheap taking his black card. I just want to not feel like these men keep buying me. Although Grams put me on the market, I'd say I'm already paid for. Don't these men want to know I'm not a gold digger?

We enter the mall and Denise tells me she usually

skips right to the top floor. She mentions how it's mostly kids stores on the first level. So we take the escalator up one floor. We start window shopping once we reach it. I get an idea on where I'd like to buy a few things.

"*Is there a Tay-Tay store here?*"

"*I believe so. We can check the board if you'd like.*"

"*We can just keep looking as we go.*"

"*Is it weird to be in a mall? I mean since you have your own clothing line?*"

"*Not at all. I like to go. Sometimes it's for inspiration and others it's to check on our displays. I do wear other people's clothes besides my own.*" We go for a little bit. "*Do you know where we are going tomorrow night? I'd like to make sure I don't over or under do it.*"

"*Oh, the formal dinner? It is for an award. We aren't sure if he's getting one or not.*"

"*And what about our reservations for tonight?*"

"*Casual. As you can tell Malcolm isn't one for suit and tie. He only wears them if he must.*"

"*Okay, gotcha.*"

"*There's a board. Let's see if that store was on it.*"

"*I see it!*"

"*Perfect.*"

We get to the display window and right away I'm not liking what I see. We enter the store and I'm trying to hide my anger from Denise. She commented on how I should be able to find the right dress here for tomorrow night. While she starts combing through the racks, I continue to make my way around the entire store. When I don't see what I'm looking for I go to the front desk.

"Excuse me, is there a manager here?"

"I'm the shift supervisor. What can I help you with?"

I am trying really hard to keep my cool. *"I was told you sell MV dresses here. Can you point me in the right direction on where they are displayed?"*

"Oh, umm, I think it's in the back right corner."

"Thank you."

I go to the back corner. How could I have missed my clothes! Okay, now I'm pissed! Five, not twenty, five of my dresses are out for sale. Tay-Tay and I have a contract and they are breaking it. I march right back up to the counter. I tap my nails on it while I wait. The girl working looks at me while she cashes someone out. The longer I stand here the angry I am getting.

"Did you find what you are looking for?"

She knows I didn't. Ugh, playing dumb is ridiculess. *"Not at all. I'm going to need to speak to the owner, right now!"*

"I'm sorry, that isn't possible."

"I am trying to be nice here because I realize you just work here. But there is a serious matter that I need to discuss with the owner."

"Ciara, is everything okay?"

"No, Denise, and I'm not leaving until it's fixed."

"What can I do to help?"

"If you'd like to go have coffee and rest your knee, I'm okay here. I have a feeling this is going to take a while."

"Oh, dear. Should I call Malcolm?"

"No. He doesn't need to be bothered." I turn my attention back to the girl. *"I don't see you getting a phone number."*

"I really don't have it."

"Call the manager, please."

I get my phone out. This girl isn't going to be of any help. Poor thing she got stuck working here today, of all days.

"Hey, Porter, I need a big favor."

"Why are you calling me? Your Grandma says I'm to hang up on you."

"If you do that, I'll fire you."

"Like I'd do that to my girl. What's up?"

"I need you to go into the computer system and pull up the contract for, hold on." I move the phone away for a second. *"What's this store number,"* I ask the girl. *"It's 45069. Got that?"*

"Yep."

"Call me back." I hang up my phone. *"You haven't called your manager yet."*

"She'll be here in five minutes."

"Great, while we wait for her, how about you go into the back room and tell me how many of my dresses are back there."

"Your dresses?"

"Yes! The MV line."

"Those are yours?"

"Yep!"

"The manager isn't going to like you!"

She hurries off to the back room. She's probably right, she isn't going to like me much. I really don't give a shit. The ones who shouldn't like me are the owners of this store. I give a huge discount to be in this store. I only do that for the front display and sixty percent of the store is supposed to be my clothing.

The owner of the store came in and she wasn't happy to learn the manager took it upon herself to display her sister's designs. How this even happened is beyond me. It's very unprofessional of the owner and the manager. The owner should know you don't just hand your baby over without keeping an eye on it. The girl that used the store to sell her sister's clothing got fired. I gotta admit it was a ballsy move, but it was a very wrong move to make. It's not the way to conduct business. You can't just go into a store and decide you're going to conduct business. It's not how it works.

For the last three hours I've been helping the owner reset the entire store. I hand-picked the gowns for the display windows and decorated them while the owner put my dresses back on the floor where they were supposed to be.

I walk out into the mall and check my windows displays. I need the storefront to be eye catching. When I like what I see, I smile

"Did you happen to find a cocktail dress while you were in there for the last three hours and twenty minutes?"

I cover my face with my hands. *"Oh my God!"*

Malcolm takes my hands from my face. *"Are you*

done? I'm a little hungry and we are late for our reservations."

"Malcolm, I'm so sorry. I saw that my brand wasn't displayed and I got upset. I had to fix it." I turn around. Denise isn't sitting on the bench anymore. I feel so bad. *"Where is Denise?"*

"I sent her home over an hour ago."

I am really going to need to make it up to Denise. Malcolm as well. I truly do feel bad. However, when your career is on the line, you can't ignore it.

CHAPTER SIX
MALCOLM

I went to my meeting and all I could think about was how beautiful Ciara is. I thought she was gorgeous in the portfolio photos, but they don't do her justice. In person she makes your heart skip a few beats. She definitely made it difficult for me to concentrate. I might have drifted off a few times thinking about her. The expression she had when I walked in on her at the bathroom door was cute. She totally had that I got caught with my hand in the cookie jar look.

I was in the meeting for just an hour when Denise sent me a text. Denise was concerned about Ciara. I excused myself so that I could call her. I knew I wouldn't be able to pay any attention to my client with such a vague text. When I stepped out into the hall, I dialed Denise's number. She sounded a little frazzled. She wasn't sure what to do. Once I found out the situation, I told her to let it be. Let Ciara deal with what needed to be done. Also, I told her to keep me updated. I went back to my meeting and made a random excuse to end this meeting. My client wasn't comprehending the security risks I found. I would have been there for hours trying to explain. I wanted to scream just let me fix the problem and we'd be done. Instead, I rescheduled the meeting. I took the rest of the week off, but it looks like I will be back in the office in a couple of days. I could have stayed, but I felt the need to be with Ciara. After all, aren't boyfriends supposed to support their girlfriend when there's a situation?

I packed up for the day and headed right to the mall. I found Denise sitting outside the store. I sat with her and watched my new girlfriend tear the clothing store apart. At first, I admired her taking a stand and fixing the problem at hand. I sent Denise home. I knew there was no reason to stick around at this point. I kept an eye on the clock. It became evident that we were not making it to our reservation.

I have to admit the longer I waited for her to finish, I was a tad bit upset. Ciara isn't here to work. I was mostly upset that we missed dinner. We lost time that we could have used to get to know each other. On top of that, Ciara didn't use her time to shop. She has no luggage with her. Come tomorrow, she won't have any clothes. Yes there is time to get a cocktail dress for tomorrow night, but I bet she won't like wearing the dress she's in again tomorrow.

Finally after hours of watching and waiting she came out of the store. She was so focused on what she was doing, she never noticed me out here sitting on my ass. Hell, she never noticed Denise was gone, either. I walked up behind her, trying to keep my cool. I asked her, *"Did you happen to find a cocktail dress while you were in there for the last three hours and twenty minutes?"* I realize I am being a jerk. She clearly got into work mode and nothing else mattered. I don't know this girl, but it seems she felt bad for ditching Denise and ruining our dinner plans.

"I'll be right back. Five minutes is all I need."

I wasn't about to let her get sucked back into working, so I followed her into the store. She goes into the back room. I wonder if I should take her back to my place now, or go out to dinner. I remind myself that I need to make a lasting impression. I know what girls want when it's been a rough day. I learned from my mother and sister what the magic cure is.

When Ciara emerges from the back room she has a garment bag in her hand. I take it from her and hold the hanger at my shoulder. *"I can carry that."*

"I got it."

"Are you hungry?"

"Yes." She smiles.

We walk through the mall side by side. I wonder if it would be weird to hold her hand. I don't want to freak her out on the first day. I also don't want her to think I'm not interested, either. I have her for a little over three weeks. I have plenty of time to hold her hand.

We drove to the restaurant and I asked her what happened. Now that I understand better what happened, I would have been pissed as well if I were her.

We get close to the place I want to take her. I want to wow her with this surprise. So I tell her to close her eyes. *"No peeking!"*

She giggles. *"Okay."*

Once I am parked I get out and open her door. I take her and guide her out. As we walk to the restaurant, I cover her eyes. I get us a table for two. I mouth to the hostess the best she has. I pull out her seat and she carefully sits down. I get real close to her ear.

"The magic cure for a bad day. I remove my hands. *"Open."*

Her eyes go wide. A smile forms and I knew I did good. *"You sure know how to please a woman."* This is just the beginning, sweet Ciara. *"You are so going to see me pig out on the first night."*

"Well, let's not waste another moment."

"Gosh, I don't know where to start."

"What's your favorite fruit?"

"Pineapple."

"Pineapple it is."

"I had no idea a place like this existed. Kind of glad we don't have one around my house, I'd be a regular customer and ask for a rewards card."

I laugh.

We get our plates and go right to the pineapple. We stab our sticks into the fruit and place them under the chocolate fondue fountain. We do about five each. While we are here, we decide to do some strawberries as well. As we sit and savor our fruit, I tell her I bring my mother and sister on their birthdays. We actually have dinner first.

"Do you want to order a meal?"

"Only if you do."

"I'm good with all this chocolate and fruit. I won't be upset if you want something more."

"I'm good just wanted to make sure this is enough."

"What's your favorite here?"

I look around. I do like the pretzels or strawberries. *"Rice Krispy treats. The chocolate makes it irresistible."*

"I'm going to get one, Mr. Miller."

I lean back in my seat and laugh. She's a very cute girl. I see she has some humor in her. She smiles when she peeks over her shoulder to me. It was damn sexy when she winked. I watch her carefully place the stick into the Rice Krispy treat. She holds it under the fountain of chocolate, making sure the entire square is covered. When she comes back, she only has one on her plate.

"I only got one in case I don't like it."

She picks it up and holds it to her mouth. I watch with hunger in my eye. A hunger for her that is. She doesn't take a bite. Instead she brings it to my lips, offering me a bite. I take a bite. My eyes pinned on hers. I return the wink she gave me.

"Delicious. You really need to try it."

She takes a bite. *"Oh, we are going to need more of this."*

"See, told ya it was good." God, help me when she moans. I need a distraction, fast. *"Okay, what's next?"*

"Oh, umm, how about black cherries."

"Okay, I'll get us some." I go and get the cherries. When I come back, I remove the stick. I hold it to her

mouth by the stem. Her teeth sink into the cherry before her red lips wrap around it. Damn, that was too hot. Who knew it would be this difficult to feed a woman chocolate covered food. My manhood is fully aware of how sexy this is. A dab of chocolate is on her bottom lip. I reach over and wipe it off with my thumb. I sure wish it were with my lips. I lick the chocolate from my thumb, wanting a taste of Ciara.

We continue to try more fruits, pretzels and even bacon. I have to admit, I did a damn good job of changing her mood and also mine. When we are full on sweets, we get a few things to take home. I could get used to this. I know it's only the first day, but I have a feeling, I want many more. We leave and she joked she doesn't have any idea where we parked since she was blinded by my hands. I put an arm around her waist and lead the way. Yep, I'm in trouble. Why did I have to be the first guy! Ten months is a long time. Time to forget me.

When we arrive at my house, it's late. I give her a quick tour. While we are in my bedroom, I give her one of my t-shirts to wear to bed. I didn't want to say goodnight, but I figured it's been a long day and she's probably tired. I walked her to her room. I told her to make herself at home before retiring to my own room for the night. I gotta tell you it was difficult to not give her a kiss goodnight. Hell, it is torture knowing a gorgeous woman is just a few feet away in another room. Honestly, I'd love to have her next to me in this big, lonely king bed of mine. It wasn't lonely until now.

CHAPTER SEVEN
CIARA

I am lying awake in Malcolm's guest bedroom. I've been trying to fall asleep, but it's difficult with being in a new place. It doesn't help that today was such a hectic day. My mind keeps reflecting on everything that went on. The flight, meeting Malcolm for the first time, and then the mall. It was enough to set my nerves on fire. Malcolm made it all worthwhile with his surprise of the chocolate fondue place. That was amazing. Nobody has ever taken the time to turn my day around the way that he did. That really meant a lot to me and showed me that he's a decent man. I can't help but wonder if that is the way he is all the time or if he wanted to impress me. Either way, he really impressed me. It means a lot that he knew just what I needed.

My first initial thought of Malcolm was that he's a very good looking man. I kind of felt like he's on the lighter side and knows how to joke around a bit. I like that about him. Laughter is needed throughout a relationship. It's nice to know that he can make me smile and laugh. But, I got to tell you he's easy on the eyes. His dark hair is kept short. He keeps a beard and mustache neatly trimmed and his light brown eyes are stunning. He's not as tall as I'd imagined he would be. He's probably 5'10-ish I'd say. Which is perfectly fine with me. I like tall men generally. He is taller than me, so it works.

I throw the blankets back, I can't lay in this bed tossing and turning anymore. My feet hit the soft carpeting. Malcolm told me I can make myself at home so maybe I'll take a gander and explore his place a little bit. I open the door slowly hoping that the door doesn't creak. Since I don't know that much about Malcolm, I'm unsure if he's a light sleeper or not. I don't want to be the one to wake him. I get out to the hallway, his room is right there. If I were the daring type, I'd knock on his door to see if he is awake. However, I'm not so daring. When it comes to men I am quite shy. I have a hard time putting myself out there because I'm always afraid of rejection. Maybe that is why all my ex-boyfriends are jerks like Hunter. Seems like I have a knack for picking the wrong man. Maybe my grandma's deceitful silent auction isn't such a bad thing after all.

I haven't moved an inch since I came out into the hallway. I keep looking at Malcolm's door, wanting to knock . I want to be daring and just go for it. After all, he didn't even try to give me a good night kiss. Did I want him to do that? Yeah, I think I did. I take a couple of steps and stop. The girl I know isn't this bold. I take a couple more steps, putting my hand on the knob. Just do it, I tell myself. I didn't even knock before inching the door open.

"Malcolm, are you awake?"

"Is everything okay?"

"Yeah, I just can't sleep."

He turns the bedside lamp on. "I have plenty of room in this big bed if you'd be more comfortable in here."

Phew, I didn't think he'd ask. I walk toward the bed. He pulls the covers back and I climb in. It's hard not to notice his bare chest. I wonder if he's fully nude. He told me he sleeps naked. Good God, what have I done? It's the first night of knowing him and I climb into his bed. I giggle to myself like a schoolgirl, thinking about how I asked Grams if I were sleeping with all ten men. I pull the covers up to my chin. I am a little embarrassed thinking about sleeping with all these men. Would that make me a slut? Do these guys think I'm going to have sex with them all? Are they going to think I'm a slut? I don't want them to think that about me. My body count isn't that high.

"Are you more comfortable?"

"Yes, thank you."

He turns the light out. *"I hope you don't snore. I'm a light sleeper."*

Well, that answered one of my questions. *"What if I do snore, is that grounds for a break-up?"*

"Hmm, that's iffy, I might have to invest in earplugs."

I giggle. *"I hope you don't snore either. I like my beauty sleep."*

"Maybe we'll snore together."

"Are you naked?" Why did that come flying out of my mouth?

"Do you want me to be naked?"

"On our first night together? What kind of girl do you think I am?"

"The kind of girl I want to know. Especially your naughty side."

We laugh at each other. *"You make me laugh. I like that about you."*

"I like you, too, Ciara."

"Good!" I roll over to my side. *"You didn't answer my question."*

"There is a way for you to find out if you want to know bad enough. Or, you could leave it to your imagination. Before you decide, there's something I want to do."

"What's that?"

"This."

He leans over and puts his lips to mine. They are soft and tender. My hand finds the back of his neck. My fingers combing through his short hair. He inches closer, I feel his silk pajama pants on my bare legs. His hand on my lower back nudges me closer to him. Our tongues slow dance together in perfect harmony. His hand slithers down further to my ass. I want him to touch me everywhere. I roll to my back, giving him the option to further explore my body. I slid my palm down his back. My fingertip, slipping into his waistband. I gasp when his fingers find my clit. I want to rip my panties off. Malcolm kisses me again. My panties getting wet the more he massages my pussy from the outside of them. If his mouth wasn't taking mine, I'd scream rip them off. It's like he read my mind when he glides his hand into the waistband of my panties. His fingers graze their way over my clit. I moan when he maneuvers his fingers into me. I slide a hand under his shirt I'm wearing and knead my breast. He works his fingers in perfect harmony setting my body on fire. I cannot control what he is doing to me. I cannot stop the orgasm from happening. I am breathless by the time my body loses control to him. He kisses me with such passion. I want more. I want Malcolm inside me.

Malcolm's upper body hovers over mine. *"That should help you sleep."* What? That's it? He doesn't want more? *"Goodnight, Ciara."*

Malcolm can't be serious right now. A guy doesn't just give an orgasm without wanting one back, right? I sure as hell haven't been with a man that does that. Hell, I've always been lucky if I cum at all. Where the hell did Grams find this man?

CHAPTER EIGHT
MALCOLM

I have been awake for hours. I already did a phone conference with the client from yesterday, so that I didn't have to do it later in the week. Now my schedule is clear again for Ciara. We have the awards ceremony tonight and I have a few things planned for the rest of the week. I haven't thought about the rest of the time just yet. I wanted to hold off to see what Ciara's interests are before I further plan our time together. I would like to see what kind of things she is into so that I get a feel if we are compatible. Relationships aren't one-sided. There are things she might want to show me.

Besides doing the conference call, I also talked with my mom. She was dying to find out how our first day went. She told me I did well with taking Ciara to the fondue place. I already knew I did, but having another woman's opinion is nice. My family all want to meet her. I decided to wait until later for that. I think Ciara and I would feel more comfortable if we knew more about each other first.

I check the time, it's getting close to ten. I ponder if I should wake her or let her sleep longer. Yesterday was a long day for her with everything that happened and traveling on top of that. I know from experience that stress can add unwanted fatigue, so maybe I should let her be. Living with someone you don't know is more difficult than I imagined it would be. For all I know, she could just be a late sleeper. Not everyone gets up at the crack of dawn as I do.

I need to find something to do with this spare time. I almost can't remember the last time I had nothing to do with my morning. Normally, I'd be at the office for hours already with my nose buried in a computer. Maybe I might have had a second coffee break by now.

I turn on my tablet that I left on the counter. I look down the hall toward my bedroom. There's no sign of Ciara waking any time soon. I start googling for something to do this coming weekend. I have an idea of what I'm looking for, but I'm not sure if I can make it happen.

"*Malcolm.*" I place the tablet face down on the counter in a hurry. I face Ciara. "*We have a bit of a problem.*"

I try to contain my laughter. "*I can see that.*"

"*I need a sewing machine.*"

"*Since I'm fresh out of one of those, I guess we need to go shopping. I seem to remember you still need clothes.*"

"*Yes, some clothes would be nice. If you do not want me to look like a clown tonight, we need a sewing machine, fast.*"

I laugh. Her dress may not fit right, but she is far from looking like a clown. The girl could probably wear a tent and I would still think she is beautiful. She tells me she is going to go get changed. I pick my tablet back up and buy tickets for this weekend, then close it out. Seeing as how Ciara already showered, she will be ready in no time.

I can now scratch going to a craft store off my bucket list of things to do before I die. Okay, it was never on my bucket list. I am not one for shopping, either. Being with Ciara has made it much more tolerable. I should have hired someone to carry the bags so that I could hold her hand instead. Maybe then it would keep the other men's eyes to themselves. It's not that I'm the jealous type, because I am not one of those guys.

"We cannot come to a mall and not get a soft pretzel."

"Your wish is granted, Ms. Verbank."

We stop and I buy a couple of soft pretzels and then we find some place to sit. I watch Ciara wipe off all the salt. I want to ask why. The salt is the best part. She then opened a mustard pack and added it to her pretzel. She looks at me and giggles. I guess she figured out I was watching her. She then holds it to my mouth. Mustard on a plain soft pretzel isn't my idea of a good mix. I appease her by trying it anyway. I have to admit it wasn't all that bad. However, it isn't as good as all the salt and nacho cheese smeared all over it. I break off a piece of mine and dip it into the cheese, holding it to her mouth. She covers her lips with her fingertips, shaking her head no.

"All is fair in love and war."

"How does that fit into this?"

"I try yours and you try mine. It's a compromising battle."

She gives me a look as if something naughty just went through her mind. *"Hmm hmm."*

"Come on, try it."

"Can I try it without all the salt?"

"What do you have against salt?"

"Nothing, I love McD's french fries." She giggles.

I take the piece I broke off for her and shove it in my mouth. I break off another piece without the salt. I lift the cheesy covered pretzel to her lips. She bites into it, her eyes close, and her moan tells me she liked it. Eating food with this woman is a difficult task at times, especially now that I know the moan matches when she orgasms. My manhood pays attention to her sweet moans and it's definitely a turn-on. I may have to start starving her in public.

"What time are we leaving tonight?"

"We have to be there by seven, so I would say by six."

She looks at her phone. *"Oh, dear, we better get going."*

"We could save you the hassle of working and buy you a new dress. There are a few designer dress shops downtown."

"I'd rather fix the one I have if you don't mind."

"I don't mind at all."

We leave the mall as soon as we finish our snack.

On the way back to my place, she asks me all about what I do. I explain the jist of my occupation to her. I don't know much about fashion and she didn't know much about mine. She proceeded to tell me how someone stole one of her designs and she believed she was hacked as she never told anyone about the design. I offered her my services. When you run a business, you need to make sure no one can steal your brand and ideas. I have done this long enough to know the internet has many security flaws. If you don't know what you are looking for, you will think you're safe.

When we get back to my place, we get her all set up in the living room since it has the best lighting with all the large windows. When I see her with a measuring tape hung around her neck, I know it's my cue to leave her to her work. I make good use of this time going over all of her files and websites. I know working isn't what we are supposed to do while we are together, but putting two workaholics together, we will find a way to do what we love most.

My mind drifts off when I see her sucking her finger after getting pricked with a needle. It makes me think about last night. It was not easy rolling over and going to sleep after giving her an orgasm with my fingers. Her scent was right there torturing me. I could have had a little taste from my fingers, but I knew it would not have been enough. I would have wanted more. I had to show a little self discipline. When the time is right, I will gladly have my way with her body.

CHAPTER NINE
CIARA

I have ripped, cut and pieced this dress back together in no time. Okay, that's not fully true, it took me longer than it should have. I kept getting distracted by taking peeks at Malcolm. He was sitting across the room, tapping his fingers on the keyboard, looking all sexy in a pair of glasses. He's already easy on the eyes, but damn did my girlie parts take notice. After that, my mind wouldn't shut off. I kept fantasizing about having him fully naked. Last night I only got to feel his upper naked body against mine. I want to feel it all. I felt his erection on my thigh and the man is definitely not lacking the goods. My curiosity is running rampant with wanting to know if he knows how to use it. Just because it's big doesn't necessarily mean he can use it.

I get into the dress and then slip into my high heels. I go to the bathroom where I left my earrings.

Malcolm comes into the room and he's dressed in a tuxedo. He comes up behind me as I put one of my earrings in. His knuckles touch my back as he zips up my dress. His mouth is so close to my ear.

"You are a stunning woman, Ciara. You are making it difficult for me to control myself. I want to take off those little purple panties you have on under this dress, lift you onto this vanity and fuck you until you give me your orgasm." I swallow the saliva in my mouth. I wouldn't deny him if he did just that. *"Unfortunately, that will have to wait. I can't blow off this event."* What a way to tease a girl, then exit the bathroom and leave a girl wanting. That was like having a cruel joke played on you.

I put my other earring in, stand up tall and run my hand down the front of my dress. I let out a deep breath and exit the bathroom as well. I walk out to the main part of the house. Malcolm is straightening his bow tie in a mirror. Payback is a bitch. I walk up behind him and reach for his tie. I am so close to his ear my lips graze them as I speak.

"It's uncomfortable."

"What is?" He asks.

"Having wet panties on." I step back, sliding my hands up under my dress. I slide my purple lace panties down my legs. I get my feet out. I stand back

up. His eyes are watching my every move. I take my panties and put them in his suit jacket pocket. *"Now there's no panties to worry about."* I walk away. I am proud of myself for being so bold and flirtatious. I just went out of my comfort zone and it felt daring as hell to do that.

Malcolm comes to where I wait by the door. *"I like this naughty side to you. I can't wait to remind you your panties are in my pocket."*

"I am looking forward to it, Mr. Miller."

All night long Malcolm has had his hand on my leg just above my knee. His thumb has been rubbing gently on my skin. It's agonizing. I want his hand to slip up under my dress, brush against my pussy and bring me to the edge of no return. I have kept my legs squeezed together for too long. Like when can we get the hell out of here?

"Care to dance with me?"

"I didn't peg you for a fast dancer."

He holds out his hand and I slip mine into his. He lifts my hand to his mouth and kisses to the top of it. He holds my hand as he leads me to the dance floor. He smiles and I return it.

"I don't fast dance."

The music changes. He puts a hand to my lower back and swings me into his embrace. I put my hands behind his neck. We sway to the music with our eyes connected. He bends, putting his forehead to mine. I shut my eyes as his lips come to mine. He kisses me in front of his friends, colleagues, and his business rivals, yet it seems we are the only ones in the room. I love feeling like I'm the only girl in Malcolm's world. How can this be real? We've only known each other for two days. If I have this connection with all ten men, I'm in trouble. If I only have this with Malcolm and we spend nine months apart will this feeling I have right now fade? I don't want this to vanish. I like being right here in his arms.

The song ends and there's an announcement that the awards are about to begin. I bite my bottom lip as we stand here gazing into each other's eyes. Can we just get the hell out of here and be the two of us already.

"Once this is over we are out of here." It's almost like Malcolm can read my mind. He leans in close. *"You see there is this girl who is pantiless and she's on the loose."*

"There is? Should we call the fashion police?"

"Nah. I think I have her in my sights."

"Do you now?" I give him a hug while I reach into his pocket. I take my panties. I step away and begin to walk away. *"Is this the way to the awards?"* I turn and dangle my panties from my finger.

"Hell ya it is."

He takes large steps as he comes after me. He takes my panties, putting them back in his pocket. I laugh. I seriously don't know who I am right now. Where has this Ciara been hiding?

We take our seats and listen to all of the awards being handed out. I take in everything that's being said. I thought this was for a remarkable job he did or something. I would have never guessed he is being recognized for being an outstanding member of the community. Malcolm takes the time to go into a vocational school once a month and teach them things he knows. I see there is still so much I need to know about this man. I have just a little over three weeks to learn everything I can.

Once again Malcolm holds out his hand for me to take. His smile is a bit devilish. Like really? He just received this amazing award and he is blowing it off like it's nothing. Is he this humble? If I were with Hunter and he was receiving this incredible award, he'd be showing it and making sure everyone knew how great he is. Hunter and Malcolm are two different men. I've been dating the wrong guy for me. I want a man who can be great and be modest at the same time. Tonight is what I needed to open my eyes. I take his hand with nothing but pure admiration. Malcolm so far is everything that I want in a man. I am so glad I did this. Grams really proved to me I was with the wrong person.

CHAPTER TEN
MALCOLM

I am so glad that the whole award thing is over. Being put on the spot like that is fine, but giving me recognition for doing something great such as teaching kids, has always been enough of an award. I don't need a piece of paper with a gold seal on it in a frame. I just need to know I helped a kid or two in their future.

"You Malcolm Miller are incredible. You act as if you don't do something good for your community."

"I don't mean to sound cocky but I do know what I do. I taught this one kid for two years. He was ambitious and wanted a good future for himself. He graduated and couldn't hack the pressure of college."

"Oh no. What happened to him?"

"He works in my office. It's been three years now. I made an impact on him and that's better than a framed piece of paper on my wall."

Ciara leaned over and kissed my cheek. *"You are a breath of fresh air."* I take her hand and interlock our fingers. She leans her head on my shoulder. *"I had a boyfriend up until this happened. The two of you are polar opposites."* I am a little taken aback by that information. How did she end up with me if she had a boyfriend already? I want to ask her if she's over him. How long ago was their breakup? *"I was furious with my grandma for going behind my back with this arrangement."*

"And now?"

"I'm still upset she went behind my back, but meeting you, I see why. Maybe understanding it is better wording. I meant what I said. You are a breath of fresh air. Whether we end up together at the end of all this or not. You showed me I deserve better. You have given me insight on the type of person I want to spend my life with."

"I haven't been in a relationship in a couple of years. Someone I know pulled the wool off my eyes of a toxic relationship."

"Who showed you you were in a toxic relationship?"

"My mother. My ex was out spending my money while I busted my ass making it. My mother saw right

through her. The money part wasn't the issue. She wasn't a very faithful person."

"I'm sorry. I'm not sure Hunter has been faithful."

"Hunter mustn't be too smart."

We arrived at my house. Ciara announces she's going to get out of her dress. Damn right she is. I haven't forgotten about her panties in my pocket. She takes the hallway toward the bedrooms. I follow her into the guest room. I walk right up behind her and unzip her dress. I slide the shoulder straps down her arms, letting my fingers softly touch her flesh. The dress gradually falls to the floor. I unhook the strapless bra and drop it to the floor next to her feet. I bend, kissing the side of her neck. I then reach up and take the pin from her hair. Her long locks fall, cascading down her back, swaying just a little bit. I put a hand to her waist and hers covers mine. Stepping forward, her naked body is touching my fully clothed body. I move her hair off to one side and kiss her neck again. Her head falls backward. I slip my hand down between her legs.

"Do you want to cum, Ciara?"

"Yes, please."

I drop my hands from her body to remove my suit

jacket. I roll my sleeves up on the white button down. She starts to turn to face me. *"Don't move,"* I order her. I take my tie off and unbutton a few buttons. I move back into position. I lift her arms and put her hands behind my neck. My finger faintly run along her arms and down her sides. Her body reacts to my touch by sucking in a breath. Her lips part as she breathes out. I run them back up to where her side meets her breasts. I skim my fingers over her nipples. A small whimper breaks out past her lips. Her nipples harden, her flesh gets goosebumps and her nails scrape my scalp. I keep teasing her body with the faintest touch. When I feel her press her body into mine more for support. I lift her into my arms, carrying her from the guest room. When I reach my bed, I lay her down. I once again run my fingers over her nipples all the way to her pussy. She spreads her legs, inviting me to her most private area. My cock twitches when I reach her clit. Climbing up onto the bed, I kiss her stomach. My mouth travels to her clit and her lower lips. I dip my tongue into her pussy.

"Mmm-hmm."

I push her thighs upward, giving me better access to her pussy. My thumb finds her clit. My tongue is as deep inside her as I can get. I lick her inner walls. I can feel her orgasm coming. I keep going until she fills my taste buds with her cum. My cock is rock hard. Throbbing to remind me that he's there ready to feel her wrapped around it's girth.

I finish taking my shirt off. I open my pants and push them down past my hips. Ciara sits up with half hooded eyes. She takes my cock into her hands, her lips brush against the head before I push her back down to the mattress. Taking hold of the backs of her thighs. I push her legs to her chest. I don't waste another second before thrusting my hips and my manhood penetrates her. I groan as her pussy takes all of me. I thrust and thrust, using her thighs to hold myself up. I am by no means being gentle. Ciara's moans tell me she doesn't mind at all. If I don't take my time, it will be over too soon. I bring her legs down and my body to hers, turning her head to kiss her. I take my time with her body instead of being a maniac.

By the time I bring Ciara to an orgasm, I am about to do the same. As much as I want to fill her with me, I can't. I pull out, get to my knees and stroke my cock. She sits up and removes my hand. She sucks my manhood into her mouth. I watch her lips wrapped around my cock. I groan. Having her sweet mouth take me throws me over the edge. I throw my head back and release my orgasm in her mouth.

I lay on the bed next to Ciara. We both stare up at

the ceiling, coming down from one hell of a night. That sex was unbelievably good. I've had great sex before with other women, but this was different. Different in a wonderful way. This connection we have is what is different for me. The chemistry we have sexually, I hope it extends out of the bedroom and she feels it as well. If not, I'm in trouble.

CHAPTER ELEVEN
CIARA

Malcolm and I have practically spent the last two days in bed. There's no denying that we have sexual chemistry together. We have more than that. And between having this great sex life we have actually been talking. I've learned more about his career that just sounds confusing to me. Computers are not my thing. Just as fashion it's not Malcolm's thing. We do share the same desires for a family. Even though Malcolm grew up in a more traditional home and I grew up with my grandma we still share the same wants. The whole husband and wife thing with two kids and maybe a dog or a cat. I want a doggy he wants a cat. But we will compromise and get a dog. Yeah he might've put up a little argument on that, but I think I could persuade him otherwise. Malcolm did ask why my Grams raised me, I felt comfortable enough sharing with him the reason why. It was not easy for me to tell him that my mother didn't know who my father was and that before I hit kindergarten my mother left me with Grams. I didn't go into much more detail than that. There's a story there that I don't fully know. I've never really had the desire to know. To me it is simple, my mother left. She didn't want to raise me, so therefore, I have no want or need to know why. My mother lost all rights to occupy my heart the moment she abandoned me. I don't think about her nor do I let her invade any part of me. That was a good enough answer for him. I'm glad it was. I don't have abandonment issues and I know that some people would think I would. Some people might even worry that I would follow in my mother's footsteps. But I won't because I want those two kids, husband, and a dog.

Today Malcolm said that he has a surprise for me. I am excited to find out what that may be. He hasn't given me much information except that I needed to pack a bag for the weekend. He did, however, tell me that we would be getting on a plane. I am not looking forward to that part only because I'm afraid to show him weakness. I don't mind flying, but I don't like the take off part of it. I keep telling myself that it's okay to have fears. I suppose if Malcolm is the guy that I end up with, he needs to know my fears. He's going to get a look at it first hand in just a few minutes.

We enter the plane and find our seats in first class. I buckle my seatbelt and make sure it's nice and tight. I lean my head back and shut my eyes, telling myself I can get through this.

"Hey, are you alright?"

"Yeah."

"You don't look okay. What's wrong?"

"I don't like when the plane takes off. I'm okay once we are in the air, even better once we land." I giggle to hide my embarrassment.

"Don't do that."

"Do what?"

"Giggle because you feel embarrassed to tell me that. You don't have to hide your emotions from me."

"Okay." I can't not do that. The whole giggle thing. It's a bad habit of mine. Sometimes I get so mad at myself for it.

"I don't like boats. I am always worried a wave will wipe us out. I don't care how big the boat is. Therefore, I've never been on a cruise ship."

I smile. *"Thank you for telling me that."*

"You are welcome." He smiles and winks at me. I watch him get out his earbuds. *"Here,"* he says, giving me half.

I put it in my ear. He turns on his playlist. *"I would not have pegged you for Native American Indian sounds."*

"It's calming. When I can't sleep, I put it on. Lean back, close your eyes and listen."

Malcolm takes my hand. His thumb is gentle when it rubs my hand. I peek at him. He, too, has his head back with his eyes closed. I smile. I breathe out a soft breath. He didn't blow my fear off as some would. He helps me through it instead just as a companion should. Where has this man been hiding? Why did I have to be auctioned off to find him? Why can't he be my only choice?

We landed in New York City. I am quite surprised by where he brought me. My home state isn't where I thought we'd end up. I do wonder why he brought me here. I am curious as to why we are staying in a fancy hotel when we could easily stay at my place. I'm not directly in the city, but I'm not far. I realize he is in control of our time together, so I'll keep my mouth shut.

"I made reservations at DeDillia's for us for six. Should I push that back a little?"

"Please don't. I'm hungry."

"I'll call for our ride then we can head down."

I use the bathroom to freshen up while he calls for our ride. I take my hair out the ponytail and finger comb my hair. That's not going to work, so I put it back. I tell myself to relax. I know the restaurant we are going to. I've been to DeDillia's a time or two. Hopefully tonight the experience will be better than those times. I also hope Hunter isn't there tonight. The few times we have dined out together, that's where we've gone. It's his favorite place to eat. The food is excellent, but Hunter's attitude made it hard to enjoy it. Every time we went there, he was quite rude to me by flirting with the waitresses.

I come out of the bathroom and Malcolm has my jacket ready for me. He holds it open while I slip my arms inside. I smile when I face him. He's a real man. He wouldn't do the things Hunter has done.

We leave and the car ride isn't far. The host sits us in a table at the window. She places our menus in front us then lights the candle on the table. Before she walks away, she asks if we'd like a bottle of the house wine of Sangiovese. Malcolm gets my approval before agreeing. We begin to look over our menu and I can't help myself when I scan the dining area. It's early so I don't think there's much of a chance of running into him. I have my fingers crossed we don't.

"You seem nervous." Am I an open book to him? How does he know me so well?

"I am."

"Do you want to leave?"

"No." I look at my menu then back to him. *"Malcolm, you know I'm from here, right?"*

"From New York, yes."

"I don't live directly in the city, but I don't live far from here. I've been here before with my ex-boyfriend. I don't want to run into him because this is where he likes to come."

"So, you do want to leave?"

"No, I just thought you should know."

"Thanks. You know that my main concern is that you are comfortable. If you are uncomfortable, I have no problems leaving."

"I'll be fine. I don't think he'll be here. Besides, the food is really good here."

The waitress comes to our table, setting down house salads, breadsticks and four of the house meatballs. We order our dinner and then dive into the appetizers. The meatballs are heavenly and the breadsticks are just as good with garlic butter. I could fill my belly with just the pre meal delights.

"Has anyone ever told you, you moan when you enjoy your food?"

I giggle. *"No. I'm sorry."*

"Don't be sorry. It's sexy as hell."

"Oh ya," I say in a flirty voice. He takes my hand and places it on the hardness in his pants. *"Oops."*

He laughs. *"Cute, Ciara."* I stroke his cock and pray nobody sees it. *"You keep that up, I'll slip my hand casually up your dress and make you cum while sitting here in a room full of people."* I raise an eyebrow. He wouldn't do that. *"Yes, I would."*

"Are you a mind reader?"

"Nah." Nah, is all he has to say?

He laughs while lifting a fork full of meatballs to my mouth. Since he silenced me. I moan. His hand comes under the table to my knee. His fingers inch their way to my thigh. I gasp. I want him to touch me. I'm not that daring though. Not yet anyway. I grab his hand and interlock our fingers. He leans back on the seat. I get a glimpse of him adjusting himself. I want to laugh, but I bite my bottom lip instead. This man makes my panties wet, my girly parts tingle and my nipples harden. I didn't know my sex drive could be this alive. I didn't know my body could respond to a man as it does to him.

The waitress takes the empty plate away, refills

our breadsticks and asks if we want the salad since we didn't touch it. Malcolm tells her we are good. She says she'll box it up for us. She fills our wine glasses before telling us our meal is almost ready. The entire time, I couldn't help but keep my eyes on him. I'm stupid for trying to catch him flirting with the waitress as Hunter would have done. Malcolm didn't ignore the girl, he looked at her to answer questions, then his attention came right back to me. Hunter would have checked her ass out as she walked away. I have truly been a fool to be with him. I wish it didn't take so long to see it. I wish Grams didn't have to show me instead of me realizing it on my own.

CHAPTER TWELVE
MALCOLM

We are walking out of DeDillia's and a man bumps into Ciara. He bumped into her hard enough, her purse fell off her shoulder. I stopped him and told him he needed to apologize, Ciara covered her mouth with her hand. Then she grabbed my arm and said it was okay. It wasn't okay for me. He was in a rush, walked into my girl and it pissed me off. When he said her name, I knew he did it on purpose. That pissed me off more.

"I think you owe the lady an apology."

"Lady, huh? Ciara, get your new boy off my nuts."

I reach out a hand and grab his peanut size nuts and squeeze. *"Don't talk to her that way. I said apologize to her."* I squeeze my hand tighter closed.

"Sorry, Ciara."

Squealing little bitch. I drop his nuts from my hand. *"Malcolm, can we go now?"* I nod my head.

"Watch yourself man, her Grandma is a snake."

Ciara spins around faster than I can stop her. *"What did you say?"*

"I said your Grams is a snake."

"Why would you say that? She never did anything to you."

"No? How about New Year's Eve night when she had a driver come to my house saying he was bringing me to the party. He offered me a drink and next thing I know, I'm at some frat house with spring chickens hanging all over me. Where were you, Ciara? I haven't heard from you since that afternoon."

"You are fucking lying. My Grandma would not do that. I called you numerous times that night. Don't blame her for getting caught with your hands in the cookie jar."

"You are delusional. Enjoy yourself, man while you can. If dear Grams don't like you, you don't have a chance."

Ciara reaches up and punches him in the jaw. Hunter doubles up his fist. He stops himself from swinging. It's a good goddamn thing he did because I wouldn't hesitate to kick his ass.

Ciara walks away, shaking out her hand. I catch up to her. *"Our car is back there."*

"I want to walk."

"Okay."

She puts her hands inside her coat pocket. It's my cue to give her time to cool off. Hunter made some serious accusations back there. Hurtful ones at that. Even I could tell his story was a bullshit one. He meant to cause pain with his words and it worked.

Ciara stops walking and looks at me. *"Can we go inside?"*

"Of course."

I hold the door open, allowing her to go first. She looks back at me with watery eyes, but smiles. I should have decked the guy. I don't like to resort to violence, but my girl is hurting he would have deserved it.

"Oh my God, Malcolm look how fucking cute these puppies are. What the heck kind are they?"

"It says they are Pomsky."

"Do you think they will let me hold one?"

"Probably. I'll go find someone who works here."

If it takes puppies to cheer her back up, puppies it will be. I find someone who works here and ask if we can see the puppies. She won't want to just hold one, so I ask for them all. He nods at me instead of using his voice. I follow him back to where Ciara is. He goes into the small room and gets two out. Then goes to another room. He comes back getting the last two.

"Follow me to the playroom. You get twenty minutes."

"Why only twenty minutes?"

"Because that's when I have to take my break."

"Oh," she replies.

We get down on the floor and start to play with the puppies. One of them isn't so playful. He or she decided to climb onto Ciara's lap and take a nap. She uses one hand to play while the other one she plays tug-a-war with a tiny rope. Two puppies fight over the rope. The last puppy is playing with a ball that I keep bouncing around. Ciara seems extremely happy again. That makes me happy.

We spent the full twenty minutes with the puppies. I could tell she didn't want to leave them. I kinda wasn't ready either. They are cute little shits for being a dog. I'm more of a cat dude. Cats need less attention. As in using a litter box instead of having to take it outside in shitty weather.

We take the car back to the hotel. On the way back Ciara told me her side of the New Year Eve party. I believe when she said she called him. I also believe her when she says her Grams wouldn't stoop that low. She ended up telling a little more of their relationship. I have to wonder why she dated someone so unappreciative of her. She's a gorgeous girl, I'm sure she gets hit on all the time. She is nice as hell. What am I missing about her that she'd lower herself to date a guy like Hunter?

We arrive at the room and I help her out of her coat. She slips out of her shoes and has a seat on the sofa. She clears her throat. *"I am not an outgoing, bold girl. I'm actually quite shy. Meeting men isn't easy for me. When I'm with you, I feel like a new person. I like who I am when I'm with you. I think Hunter took my kindness and shyness as a weakness. Therefore, he could be an ass, I guess. I allowed him to be that way."*

"He didn't treat you the way a woman should be treated when in a loving relationship, no matter if you are shy or outgoing. He's a bully in a way, and he's the one that is weak not you."

"I know it's wrong, but it felt really good to punch him."

I pat my coat pockets. *"I left my credit card at the restaurant. I'm going to run back and get it."*

"You don't mind if I stay here do you?"

"Not at all. You might want to ice your knuckles there slugger." She laughs. I give her a kiss. *"I'll be right back. Need anything while I'm out?"*

"No, I'm good."

I leave the hotel. I didn't leave my credit card at DeDillia's as I told Ciara. I am going back to the restaurant, though. She didn't need to know I have a few choice words for her ex. I should have stood up to him earlier. She pretty much didn't need me to, though. She says she is not a bold girl. I think it was pretty damn bold to clock him in the jaw.

I walk into the restaurant and find Hunter at the bar with his arm swooped over some lady. Poor woman doesn't have a clue what kind of guy he is. I tap him on the shoulder. He gives me a look.

"What now? Did the princess kick you to the curb?"

"Mind if we have a word in private?"

"I kinda do mind. In case you are blind. I'm with friends."

"I don't care for the way you talked to my girlfriend earlier nor do I like that you thought about punching her."

The girl he has his arm draped over asks, *"Hunter, what is he talking about?"*

"Nothing, baby. Don't pay attention to him."

"Actually, you should listen up. Hunter here almost hit my girl after he ran his mouth and she gave him that bruise forming on his jaw." She takes his arm off her shoulders.

"What the fuck is your problem? I don't even know you."

"When you bump into a lady, you should say you're sorry. Instead you verbally attacked Ciara then you actually wanted to hit her. My problem is nobody is going to get away with mistreating a woman when I'm around."

"Go back to your new woman and mind your damn business. You'll see one day how great it is to be with her. Christ, the girl isn't even a good enough fuck to deal with her Grandma. She's yours, run along now."

Ciara is right about one thing. It felt good punching him. I shake out my fist while he drags himself off the floor. He yells for someone to call the cops. The girl he was with, slaps him across the face. I glance at his hand balled into a fist. *"Go for it, buddy. I'll gladly hit you again."*

"Is anyone going to call the cops? You are all my witness, he hit me."

Everyone goes back to doing what they were before I walked in causing enough of a commotion with my voice. No one is going to side with him. I turn away and make my way outside. I smile because Damn that felt good. I look at my knuckles. Now I might need a little ice.

CHAPTER THIRTEEN
CIARA

I jump up from the sofa when I hear the hotel room's door unlock. Malcolm has been gone longer than I expected he would be. I really hope he didn't run into Hunter again when he went back. I don't want Malcolm to feel like he needs to fight my battles. I can take care of myself, so it seems. I have never hit a person before, but damn did I land a good punch to his face.

"Sorry it took longer than I planned. I got you something."

I smile like a little girl. *"What's underneath your coat?"* He pulls back the front panel of his coat. My eyes go wide. *"You didn't!"*

"I did!"

I do a little happy dance. *"What's its name?"*

"I don't know, you tell me."

"Shut up, this really isn't a puppy for me."

"Yes it is. She's all yours."

I go and take my gift from him and hug this ball of fur. I give Malcolm a kiss. *"I can't believe you did this."*

"I couldn't resist after seeing her sleeping on your lap."

I walk back to the couch. *"We need to go shopping for all kinds of doggy stuff. I'm totally blinging out her stuff."*

"I wasn't sure what you'd want, so I only bought a few things. Just enough to get by until you get whatever you want for her."

"You didn't have to do this. This dog was over a thousand dollars. I can pay you for her."

"You will do no such thing. I wanted to do it or else I wouldn't have done it."

"Thank you so much. It's one of the sweetest things anyone has ever done for me." I pet my pup. *"You know, I thought you went back to confront Hunter."*

"I might have done that too."

"What happened?"

He shows me his red knuckles. *"It was very satisfying."*

"Did he hit you back?"

"Not when I knocked him to the floor."

"Damn, remind me to never hit you."

"Ciara, you know I'd never raise a fist to you as he did, right?"

"Yeah, I know." I bring my new puppy to my face and kiss her. *"You need a name."*

"How about Fluffball?"

I laugh. *"Yeah, no. Her name needs to be cool."*

My puppy settles on my lap. I really cannot believe he did this. I've always wanted a dog, but Grams gave me a firm no on that. She always said we travel too much for that.

I lean my head on Malcolm's shoulder and pet my new baby. *"Any idea what you want to name her?"*

"Not yet. She must have husky in her. She has the blue eyes a husky would have and the markings."

We google the breed and then google some names. Nothing is popping out at me. Our conversation changes and we start talking about places we've traveled to. Then I ask Malcolm a serious question.

"If we end up together, where would we live? Your business is in California and mine is here."

"We could travel back and forth together between the two places until we figure it out."

"Do you want to be with me?"

"So far, yeah I do. We are still getting to know one

another. Nine months is also a long time to be apart. You will be with other men that might capture your heart."

"What if I don't want to even date the other men? I could just be with you."

"I'd be selfish if I told you to forget them and just choose me. I care enough for you that I want you to be happy. I didn't want to be the first guy you dated because if I had true feelings for you and then you didn't choose me, in the end I'd be the one left hurt. There's this huge chance you'd forget all about what we share."

"There's no way I'll forget about you, Malcolm. I don't want to be the reason you end up hurt."

"When I signed up for this, it's a chance I was willing to take. Who knows in the next two weeks, you may not even like me anymore."

"I don't see that as a possibility."

"Only time will tell, right?"

"Ya, I guess."

"Are you ready to get some sleep?"

"Yes, it's been a long day."

"I'm going to take the pup outside before we turn in."

"I think I'm going to shower."

Malcolm gets up, gives me a kiss then takes the

puppy off my lap. His hand cups my jaw, and he tells me to not think about the next nine months. I think I've come to know him well enough, he thinks about it as much as I do. I can't not think about it. It's hard knowing we have this amazing connection and we will part ways in two weeks. Honestly, I'm not sure I can walk away from such an amazing guy.

Once Malcolm leaves, I sit here a little longer. My stomach is suddenly in knots. I think I fell hard and fast for him. I think I'm in love with him. I'd be a fool if I weren't. He's truly an all-around great guy. Is it even possible to love someone this quick? It happens, right? It's never happened for me, but to other people it has.

I get up from the sofa and head for the shower. I just don't know how my heart can handle this. I don't think Grams realizes how this is going to affect me and everyone involved. I could be the one crushing someone's heart or hell, it could be mine crushed in the end. Who's to say in the end I end up with my choice. In nine months from now, if I pick Malcolm, there's no guarantee he'll wait for me. There's no way of knowing if he'll even look at me the same after dating nine other men.

My eyes well up with tears. The thought of Malcolm looking at me in any other way is upsetting.

I put my face under the shower, letting the water cascade down my face. I wish it could wash away the teardrops that are falling. Malcolm gets in the shower behind me. I turn and throw myself into his arms.

"*I can't bear the thought of hurting you. I don't want to be the reason you don't get what you deserve.*"

"*Sweetheart, please don't cry. I signed up for this knowing that I could end up alone. Wherever this journey leads you, just follow your heart. That's all I ask of you.*"

"*You might be stronger emotionally than I am. I can't flip a switch and turn off these feelings I already have for you.*"

"*We will get through this, okay? With you showing me your emotions, shows me you care. That's enough for me right now.*"

"*What if I'm falling in love with you already?*"

"*Then we have two more amazing weeks ahead of us. If loving each other is right, nine months won't stand a chance against that.*"

I get up on my tiptoes and kiss Malcolm. This man makes me feel so much. He makes me feel loved. I see now I was never treated the way I should have been. My past relationships were all wrong. I just want to stay here with him.

"Make love to me, Malcolm."

He reaches for the knobs to turn the water off. He then gets out, I follow him. When he sweeps me off my feet and carries my wet body to the bed, I bury my face in his neck. I think I really am in love with him.

CHAPTER FOURTEEN
MALCOLM

My time with Ciara is coming to an end. These past three and half weeks have gone by too fast. I have to put her on a plane back to New York in just two hours. I don't want to do it. I want to scream, stay with me, marry me and build a life together. I know it's not what I signed up for. I have to let her go and pray she comes back to me.

I have to admit, I didn't honestly think I would fall for a girl who's Grandma auctioned her off. I don't know what I was thinking would happen. I do know, these past weeks I fell for one incredible lady. She is funny, sweet and caring. Not to mention sexy as fuck. Our sex life is simply amazing but there's so much more to her than sex. I learned she is one hell of a designer. When we went to New York City, I bought us tickets to a fashion show. She was so passionate about all of it. To me they were just clothes. To Ciara they are art. After the show, we spent two days at her home. I saw her boutique, met her friend Porter and saw inside her world. I also met her Grandma, who seems to have Ciara's best interest at heart. I can see myself fitting nicely into her world. After that we came back to my home. She accompanied me to work a couple of times. She took a general interest in my world. That was very pleasing. I have to say, I knew I was in trouble when I took her to meet my family. That was when I knew for sure I was in love. Ciara fit perfectly with my family. They love her and she loved them. There's no denying our lives mesh very well together. I hate knowing I have to wait nine months to see if our love can stand the test of time.

"What are you thinking about?"

"How much this fucking sucks."

I take Ciara's hand, stopping her from putting more clothes in her luggage. *"I figured."*

"I don't understand why you want me to go through with this."

"I don't understand it, either."

"You love me, right?"

"Yes."

"Then why? Why send me into another man's arms?"

"I once read, if you love something, set it free and if it comes back it is yours."

"You don't have to do that. I'm already yours."

"Trust me, Ciara, putting you on a plane to send you home, is the last thing I want to do right now."

"Then don't do it."

"You know I have to. It was all in the agreement."

"I never agreed to this. My Grandma did all this without my knowledge."

"You agreed to it the moment you got on the plane to meet me. I don't like it any more than you do."

"You're not even going to fight for me?"

"I didn't say that. I am not giving up what we have. I'm sure not going to let you forget me, either."

"You're not allowed to keep in touch with me."

"Every time you pet Alaska, feed her, talk to her, is a reminder of who gave you that dog. I'm going to be with you for as long as you own her."

"It's not the same." I pick up a stack of clothes. *"I have to finish packing."*

"Ciara, look at me." Her eyes fill with tears. *"I do love you. I didn't think it would be possible. I'm not going anywhere. I'll be right here in nine months."*

"I hope I will be too. If I hurt you, just remember you didn't keep me."

"I am keeping you." I lift her hand to my chest, putting it over the heart that is pounding furiously for her. *"I am keeping what we have right here. I hope you do the same for me."*

"I'd like to go now, please."

"We have another hour before we need to leave."

"It's too hard. Why drag out our goodbye and see you in nine months, maybe any longer?" She closes her suitcase.

"I'll get the car ready." I grab the stuff off my bed.

I don't like this any more than she does. It's literally tearing my heart out, but I cannot show her that. For the life of me, I cannot figure out why I'm letting her go. Maybe in my subconscious mind I want to know that she picks me on her own and not because I put a bid in on dating her. Come November I want her to choose me over everyone else. Choose us.

We arrive at the airport, and I walk Ciara in. She goes to check in and I hold Alaska while she does. I have a talk with the dog that I purposely bought to make her think of me every damn day she's gone. I hold the puppy up to my face. *"It's*

your job to remind her of me. Love her for me in my absence and come home to me. My arms will be wide open for you both."

"I'm all checked in."

My head is screaming inside to not let her go. I put Alaska in her carrying bag. I stand and bring Ciara into my arms. I kiss her head. *"I love you, Ciara. Come back to me."*

She pushes away from my chest. She places her hand to my cheek. She smiles a smile that is filled with sadness. I close my eyes as tears drip down onto my cheek. *"I love you, too, Malcolm."*

Her thumb wipes away my tears. She steps out of my arms and wipes her own away. She picks up the dog bag and puts it on her forearm. She doesn't say goodbye. She doesn't say anything at all. I stand here feeling my heart walk away. I hope she brings it back.

About the Author

Thank you so much for taking the time to read Grandma's Silent Auction January. Word-of-mouth is crucial for any author to succeed. If you enjoyed the book, please leave a review on Amazon. Even if it's just a sentence or two. It would make all the difference and would be very much appreciated. – OXOX Michael James

Website: http://michaeljames-author332.bravesites.com/

Also by MICHAEL JAMES

If you enjoyed Grandma's Silent Auction January, you may also like my other books:

The Way We Love series:

Pink Skies At Night

Shadows At Night

Nights Are Unlimited

Concealed By The Night

Shattered At Night

Freed At Night

Winning A Cowgirl's Heart - Trilogy:

The Rodeo King

The Best Friend

The Fate Of My Heart

Winning a Cowgirl's Heart -Complete Box Set

Construction Vs. Corporate- Trilogy:

Unbalanced

Balancing

Balanced

Secrets Within a Club

Club Comrade

Revenge

Saving Club Conrad

Masquerade Saga

His Pearls

His Secrets

His Prison

His Games

His Moves

All His

Crime in Landkaster series

The Mirror

Times Like These

Standalone:

Toying With October

Pieces Of Me

A Christmas For Eve

Dom Diaries: Tangled Up In You

Christmas Scavenger Hunt

Blue Christmas

Stealing the Christmas Spotlight

Co-written with Jodi Fahey

Last Sheet

Manufactured by Amazon.ca
Bolton, ON

43907260R00063